# OVERVIEW OF SEEKER EVANGELISM IN DISCIPLING MUSLIM BACKGROUND BELIEVERS

Abu Da'ud

**Overview of Seeker Evangelism in Discipling Muslim Background Believers**

Copyright © 2019 by Abu Da'ud

All rights reserved. No part of this publication may be reproduced, stored in a retrieval system, or transmitted in any form by any means, electronic, mechanical, photocopy, recording or otherwise, without the prior written permission of the publisher, Abu Da'ud, except as provided for in the copyright law of the United States of America.

ISBN: 978-1-950254-12-5

eISBN: 978-1-950254-13-2

eISBN: 978-1-950254-14-9

All Bible quotations are from the World English Bible, which is not copyrighted. It is in the public domain for both print and electronic formats.

# Table of Contents

Introduction ........................................................... 1

1   Muslim Ministry ............................................. 5

   1.1   Diagnostic Questions ............................. 8

2   Choosing Evangelism Methods ................... 13

   2.1   Jesus Is a Gift ....................................... 13

3   Clearing Up a Seeker's Misconceptions About Christianity ....................................................... 23

4   How I Came to Understand the Truth of the Gospel – and Found an Evangelism Method That Works with Muslims ............................................................. 51

   4.1   I Had Three Questions Before Becoming a Christian ................................................ 52

   4.2   I Knew God Existed ............................. 53

   4.3   I Felt That God Would Remain a Mystery ......... 55

   4.4   My Concept of God Prior to Becoming a Christian 56

   4.5   The Three Main Religions, Islam, Judaism, and Christianity, Cannot Be Reconciled with Each Other ... 57

   *4.6*   *Star Wars* ............................................. 58

   4.7   My First Question Answered – The Virgin Birth 59

   4.8   My Second Question Answered – The Trinity ... 59

   4.9   My Third Question Answered – Jesus Is the Son of God ................................................... 62

   4.10   My Salvation ....................................... 76

| | | |
|---|---|---|
| 5 | Preparing Your Knowledge Base | 79 |
| 6 | Some More Evangelism Methods | 83 |
| 7 | Considerations for the Seeker | 97 |
| | 7.1 Ask for Revelation | 97 |
| | 7.2 Become Familiar with Essential Christian Beliefs | 98 |
| | 7.3 What Does Being a Christian Look Like? | 101 |
| | 7.4 Counting the Cost | 106 |
| | 7.5 Some Significant Differences Between the Quran and the Bible | 107 |
| 8 | Prayer for Salvation | 113 |
| 9 | Steps to Take After Salvation | 117 |
| Books | | 121 |
| About the Author | | 127 |

# **INTRODUCTION**

This book, which accompanies the Muslim ministry handbook *Discipling Muslim Background Believers*, provides an overview of the handbook's sections on evangelizing Muslim seekers. It describes ways to lead a Muslim to salvation in Jesus Christ. However, it will not provide the seeker with the ability to answer critical questions independently – *Discipling Muslim Background Believers* will do that.

*Discipling Muslim Background Believers* is in an easily-referenced handbook format, providing a Muslim background believer ("MBB") with practical advice from an MBB about living a biblically-based Christian life in a Muslim context. Some of the guidance in the handbook covers:

- praying, reading and understanding the Bible

- correcting MBB misconceptions about Christianity
- engaging in spiritual warfare
- family life and relationships
- evangelism and discipleship, and
- starting and growing small groups and churches

In addition to this book, I recommend using both *Discipling Muslim Background Believers* and the accompanying Bible study – *Muslim Seeker Bible Study* – with the seeker. The Bible study highlights important Bible verses and will also specifically refer to sections in the handbook for further study.

If you are unfamiliar with Islamic beliefs, please research the six articles of belief and the five pillars of Islam by clicking on the appropriate link on the blog page of my website, abudaud.com.

This book does not contain legal, psychological or medical advice. None of the suggestions are intended as guarantees that you will experience any type of intended result.

Bold text is used in body paragraphs in this book to indicate concepts or phrases dealt with more fully in *Discipling Muslim Background Believers*.

# 1   MUSLIM MINISTRY

Christian ministry around the world has enjoyed great success. However, areas of unrealized potential remain. Christian ministers in Muslim communities often encounter strong resistance to the gospel. While Muslim ministry may seem difficult to many Christians, that difficulty can be partially overcome through spiritual preparation and good understanding. Islam is a meta-culture. Though Muslim-majority countries differ greatly, their societal and individual responses to the gospel and to an MBB are often more strongly driven by Islam than by a national culture.

There are two main branches of Islam: Sunni and Shia. The Sunni believe that people come to Islam through faith, whereas the Shia claim a lineage to Muhammad. The Sunni claim that Ali was the fourth caliph, while Shia claim he was the first. Also, the Shia believe that the Mahdi will come to establish Islam across the world, with Jesus acting in support of his efforts. There are other differences. However, in my experience, the responses to the gospel from both Sunni and Shia are essentially the same. The Quran teaches Muslims how to respond to Christians.

Muslims differ in their view of the Quran. Some see it promoting peace while others see it promoting war. These differences do not seem to be the determinants of how Muslims react to the gospel. While they may be outwardly open to Christians, some peaceable Muslims are more resistant to the gospel than even jihadists. Thus, the factors of type of Islam and level of extremism do not seem to be the determining factors regarding openness to the gospel.

In my experience, the two main factors seem to be: 1) the degree of openness to new ideas; and 2) the degree of willingness to think independently. The more open a person is to new ideas and the more willing to think independently, the easier it is to present the gospel and see a successful outcome. Diagnostic questions can be asked to determine the seekers degree of openness, but please spiritually prepare yourself first.

The following activities should be done as spiritual preparation before **sharing the gospel** with Muslims, sometimes more than once:

- **prayer**
- **prayer walking**
- **spiritual mapping**
- **spiritual warfare**
- **fasting**.

Below are some diagnostic questions that can help a Christian determine how open a Muslim is to the gospel, allowing the Christian to tailor an approach for a particular Muslim.

## 1.1 DIAGNOSTIC QUESTIONS

Muslims often cling to the tradition of Islam because of the importance of Islamic culture, familial traditions and the individual's own views of God. You can frame questions to determine the strength of these barriers in the listener by asking things like:

- Do you have a personal relationship with God?

    **[If yes]** Please tell me about it. (Would you mind telling me about it?)

    **[If no]** Would you like to have a personal relationship with God?

- Is your view of God based mainly on what you have heard from others or your own thinking/study/research? On a scale of 1-10 (10 being completely based on your efforts), how much is based on your own thinking/study/research?

- Does your family (tribe, culture, country, town or village) feel the same way about God?

    You can also ask the same question about parents, brothers, sisters, etc.

- How would they react if someone left the family (tribe, culture, country, town or village) religion?

The answers to the above can help the MBB better understand the listener's mindset. They can also be used to find **similarly situated MBBs**.

Muslims may be prepared for your **evangelism** approach. The Quran and its regulations, the hadith, prescribe large parts of the daily life of a Muslim. The Quran contains specific answers to give to Christians sharing the gospel, and Muslims families teach these responses to their children. Some examples include the following verses in the Quran: 2.97-101, 2.111-112, 2.213-214, 3.18-20, 3.64-71, 3.72-80, 3.98-101, 4.153 4.171, 5.15-19, 5.59, 5.67-69, 5.77-80, and 29:45-49. Muslims are trained to respond to Christians using a prepared script. Familiarity with these passages will prepare you to answer them.

By God's grace I have personally helped over fifty Muslims pray the prayer for salvation, and even more responded in group responses to gospel presentations. Telling stories, yours or those from the Bible, and asking the right type of questions avoids the trap of following the Muslims' script.

There is no requirement to follow their script. In fact, following their lead and trying to directly contradict their many assertions usually leads to fruitless arguments that can last many hours and even eventually spread over many days as the discussions continue each time you meet.

Rather than responding, change the script. This means that the Muslim will now actually have to think rather than rely on prepared answers, giving you the opportunity to present truth that can actually be impactful because the Muslim will now be listening. The discussion becomes a real dialogue at this point.

# 2  CHOOSING EVANGELISM METHODS

One method of sharing the gospel that can work with most Muslims is below.

## 2.1  JESUS IS A GIFT

Many Christian efforts to evangelize Muslims end up in fruitless arguments because Christians and Muslims do not have common grounds for understanding God or how to relate to Him. Sharing the gospel with Muslims without overtly referring to the Bible or the Quran, neither of which is accepted as true by adherents of the other faith. Muslims actively train to deflect overtly Bible-based evangelism methods. Are there simple yet effective evangelism methods that share common ground without compromising the Bible? Yes.

One method you can use involves two gift analogies. It requires only a shared knowledge of the basics of gift-giving and inheritance, things that almost every culture knows and understands. Using the method works for me, and has worked for people to whom I have taught it. Using the method also gives the Muslim an impetus to respond to the presentation, either by receiving Jesus Christ as Lord and Savior or by praying to receive a revelation about God's true nature. The method is very flexible because it does not require memorizing a script.

The first analogy is the general idea of giving gifts. Most cultures give gifts, and Muslims are no exception. In fact, gift-giving is an important aspect of Muslim culture. Gifts in the Muslim world mean many things, but they commonly show hospitality and care for the recipient.

The practice of gift-giving can be used to communicate the gospel using an analogy based on something deeply ingrained in the hearer's culture. The analogy can be framed in different ways, but these are the basics:

1. If the giver gives a gift of little value to the giver and the intended recipient refused it, then there is little if any negative effect on the relationship between giver and recipient. An example is refusing a piece of offered chewing gum. The refusal would not be given a second thought, and the relationship would be unaffected.
2. However, if the giver put all of himself into the gift and the intended recipient refuses it, then there can be little or no relationship because the intended recipient refused the giver—not just the gift. An example is a man's engagement gift to his fiancé. Her refusal of the gift would

definitely change the relationship and prevent the offered closeness.

The analogy can then be applied to the seeker's decision about whether to follow Jesus as Lord and Savior. First, present the contrast in the numbered paragraphs above. Then mention that the triune God put Himself completely into Jesus and made it clear that He did so, offering Jesus as a gift to us as a way to know God and be forgiven of sin. Thus, rejecting Jesus means that the intended recipient of the gift cannot have a relationship with God. In fact, the only way to have a relationship with God would be to receive His gift. Far from being harsh or unfair, the giving of this gift is marvelous because it is freely offered to those who do not honor or follow God at the time of the gift. Receiving the gift is the way to be cleansed of sin and to enter into relationship with God. Since Muslims are quite attuned to the idea of submission –

"Islam" means submission – it is easy to then tell them that the way to receive this gift is to repent of sin and to fully submit one's life to God the Father through God the Son. Muslims may balk at the idea of accepting the Son of God. If they continue to do so after careful explanation, Chapters 3, 4, 6 and 7 may be useful. There is a prayer mentioned below that is also very helpful.

The other analogy in the method is that of receiving an inheritance. An inheritance can only be received if a person is mentioned in the will – usually just family members. The obvious application is that the seeker must actively repent and receive Jesus as Lord and Savior to be part of God's family and live with Him forever.

The gift analogy can be used with Muslims not only if they want to know why Jesus is the only way but also to show them the importance of immediately responding positively once they see the truth of Jesus' deity. Since most Muslims enjoy talking about God and many enjoy logical debate, a useful tool is to use the analogy or analogies above within a hypothetical. You can ask the Muslim to hypothesize that Jesus is God, then present the analogy. The truth of Jesus' claim to be the only way becomes evident – He's God and is the only way to relationship and forgiveness because He is the fullness of God and paid the price for our sins. Also, at least two reasons for an immediate response also become clear. First, since Jesus is God and is offering Himself as the only way, He should not be refused even for a moment. Second, once you convince the seeker that Jesus is the only way, there is no reason for the seeker to postpone even a moment of the blessing of knowing God, who is loving, merciful, kind and compassionate.

I used this method on myself a week before I was saved and was absolutely stunned. I reasoned that if indeed He was God, then I could not really refuse to follow Jesus because I wanted to follow God. For the first time I could see the choice plainly – accept the gift of Jesus or reject a relationship with God. Also, I could see the surpassing glory of God's gift. He was offering me Himself and a place in His family. So, if indeed Jesus was the gift, my only logical choice would be to follow Him, the one who is God and at the same time the gift of God. My problem was that I could not come to grips with the idea that Jesus was God – God in the flesh. I knew that God could put Himself into a man because He was all powerful. The analogy showed me why He might do it – to give man an obvious and simple way to come to Him—to receive His inheritance—that truly depended on God's goodness rather than man's effort. I did not want to accept that God was actually offering me Himself at that time because I felt that I did not have enough evidence yet about the identity of Jesus.

I had stubbornly maintained my stance of not wanting to become a Christian. However, I was having severe problems with that stance because of the stunning simplicity, beauty and power I saw in God's nature and Jesus' nature if the analogy of the gift was a representation of reality. I just was not sure that God had actually come in the flesh. This is a common barrier for a Muslim seeker, and often has a common solution—invite the seeker to pray a simple but powerful prayer.

When sharing the gospel, if the Muslim seeker does not want to receive Jesus Christ as Lord and Savior at that moment, you can ask if the seeker fully trusts God to be good, kind and true. Once the Muslim answers affirmatively, you should ask the Muslim to pray to God and ask Him to reveal to the seeker who He truly is. The understanding should be that the seeker will follow what is revealed. If prayed sincerely, God will reveal Himself.

I prayed that prayer more than thirty years ago after considering the two analogies. He revealed Himself powerfully, and I began to follow Jesus as my Lord and

Savior. I am grateful that He made it possible for me to be part of His family.

Please note that there are more evangelism methods in Chapters 4 and 7.

# 3   CLEARING UP A SEEKER'S MISCONCEPTIONS ABOUT CHRISTIANITY

Below are some basic truths about Christianity that clear up common Muslim misconceptions about Christianity.

**God** is the **Father**, **Son** and **Holy Spirit**, the one true God who is one essence in three persons – the **Trinity**. Each of the three have the same essence and attributes, and are each persons as we are persons. The exception to that description of personhood is that our personhood has a separate identity. God's single identity is made up of three persons that can each recognize the other two as separate persons.

God is. He is self-existent. He revealed Himself as such when He revealed the name: I Am. The name is represented by YHWH in English transliteration. It is also represented by Yahweh, Jehovah, and Lord (Adonai).

Jesus is the Word of God. He existed for all of time and even before it as is shown in the following passage:

> [1] In the beginning was the Word, and the Word was with God, and the Word was God. [2] The same was in the beginning with God. [3] All things were made through him. Without him was not anything made that has been made. John 1:1-3 WEB

Jesus was always with God and was not created. All things created came into being through Him.

One of the characteristics of God is that He loves us. I knew that about Him before becoming a Christian. However, I did not understand that He is love.

> …. for God is love. 1 John 4:8 WEB

For God, love is not just what He does. It is who He is. Love, among other things, chooses to do for others what is best for them. It seeks to give of itself to another without setting conditions, seeking a relationship *for the benefit of the other*. Love gives unconditionally to benefit the other, not itself. That is what God the Father does, as do the Son and Holy Spirit. I believe that is why God created mankind – He wanted to love people and bless people. He was neither lonely nor needy. He did not have a need to give anything nor benefit nor receive anything – He wanted to bless mankind and **bring them into His family**.

The Bible tells us how love acts:

[4] Love is patient and is kind; love doesn't envy. Love doesn't brag, is not proud, [5] doesn't behave itself inappropriately, doesn't seek its own way, is

> not provoked, takes no account of evil; doesn't rejoice in unrighteousness, but rejoices with the truth; **⁷** bears all things, believes all things, hopes all things, endures all things. **⁸** Love never fails..... 1 Corinthians 13:4-8a WEB

The positive elements of the passage describe ways God acts towards those He loves.

God is a father in that He created us all. He includes in His family those who follow Jesus Christ the Messiah as Lord and Savior.

The Father is listed first when the whole Trinity is mentioned in the New Testament. An example follows:

> **¹⁹** Go, and make disciples of all nations, baptizing them in the name of the Father and of the Son and of the Holy Spirit, .... Matthew 28:19 WEB

He is Creator.

¹ In the beginning, God created the heavens and the earth. ² The earth was formless and empty. Darkness was on the surface of the deep and God's Spirit was hovering over the surface of the waters.
³ God said, "Let there be light," and there was light.
Genesis 1:1-3 WEB

These verses show the action of God the Father, Son and Holy Spirit, the one true God who is one essence in three persons.

Jesus is the Word of God. In verse 3 above, He is shown to be there when God speaks. The following verses from the New Testament show He was there the whole time, from the beginning:

¹ In the beginning was the Word, and the Word was with God, and the Word was God. ² The same was in the beginning with God. ³ All things were made through him. Without him was not anything made that has been made.  John 1:1-3 WEB

God the Father is perfectly just:

⁷ But Yahweh reigns forever.
He has prepared his throne for judgment.
⁸ He will judge the world in righteousness.
He will administer judgment to the peoples in uprightness.  Psalm 9:7-8 WEB

The penalty for Adam's sin was severe:

¹² Therefore as sin entered into the world through one man, and death through sin; and so death passed to all men, because all sinned.  Romans 5:12 WEB

All mankind should die as a result of **sin**.  God could not let sin go unpunished because that would violate His just demands.  While He is merciful, He must also satisfy His just nature.  He did so.

²³ For the wages of sin is death, but the free gift of God is eternal life in Christ Jesus our Lord.  Romans 6:23 WEB

Jesus Christ the Messiah, the Son of God, who is God and also the second person of the Trinity, gave His life to pay for the life of every person.  God the Holy Spirit raised Him from the dead.  Those actions satisfied both justice and mercy because sin was paid for and the way to **salvation** was open through Jesus Christ the Messiah.

God the Father has many feelings, including wrath and anger, but He is also compassionate, touched by our pain and sorrow. He demonstrates His love and He rejoices over His own in unabashed displays of affection.

> [17] Yahweh, your God, is among you, a mighty one who will save. He will rejoice over you with joy. He will calm you in his love. He will rejoice over you with singing. Zephaniah 3:17 WEB

God the Father is the God of Abraham, Isaac and Jacob. There are many references to this in the Bible, including the following example from the revelation of God to Moses:

**⁶** Moreover he said, "I am the God of your father, the God of Abraham, the God of Isaac, and the God of Jacob."

Moses hid his face; for he was afraid to look at God.
Exodus 3:6 WEB

People make much of whether followers of Jesus Christ the Messiah as Lord and Savior from Muslim backgrounds can refer to God as Allah, since Allah is originally a pagan name.  The objection is often raised by English speakers who refer to the Creator as "God", which also has pagan roots.  The main thing about word choice is intent.  God knows your heart, so feel free to call Him Allah if you choose, as long as you are intending, after becoming a Christian, to address the Father, Son and Holy Spirit.  It may be useful to call Him Allah if you need to be a **secret believer**.  By the way, "Khoda" is originally Zoroastrian – the same reasoning applies.

Regardless of the name you choose, the Father, Son and Holy Spirit are definitely not the same as the God portrayed in Islam. Islam denies the deity of Jesus, denies that the Holy Spirit is a separate person but the same essence as God and says that Christians worship three gods. Christians believe that the Father, Son and Holy Spirit are three persons with one essence, one identity – one God. Islam denies that Jesus died on the cross and denies the resurrection. In Islam, you can go to heaven if your good deeds outweigh your bad and Allah wills it. In Christianity, Jesus Christ the Messiah is the only way to salvation.

From the few differences above it is easy to see that the Allah of Islam is not the same as the Creator portrayed in Christianity. If an MBB decides to call the Creator Allah, that is acceptable as long as contradictory thoughts and patterns from Islam are not allowed to mix with your new theology (*see* **syncretism**).

Jesus is the second person of the Trinity. Jesus is listed second when the whole Trinity is mentioned in the New Testament.

> ¹⁹ Go, and make disciples of all nations, baptizing them in the name of the Father and of the Son and of the Holy Spirit, …. Matthew 28:19 WEB

Jesus is the second Person of the Trinity. The following verse gives insight into Jesus' nature:

> ⁹ For in him all the fullness of the Godhead dwells bodily, …. Colossians 2:9 WEB

This verse shows that Jesus is the embodiment of all of God. Therefore, the nature and character revealed by every name of God applies to Jesus. It could be said that every name of God applies to Jesus except those that specifically refer only to the other two distinct persons of the Trinity. For example, Jesus cannot be referred to as the "Father" or "the Holy Spirit", though He said He and the Father were one. To do so would cause be inaccurate and confusion.

Note that Jesus was fully God and fully man. He came here in flesh, not as representation of it. Coming in the flesh is also referred to as incarnation.

Jesus fulfilled many prophecies, all of which were made more than 400 years before He was born. Rather than reiterate what has been dealt with very well by others, three of the many excellent books that cover the subject as part of their content are recommended:

1. Josh McDowell, *Evidence That Demands A Verdict* (first printing 1972);
2. Lee Strobel, *The Case for Christ*
3. Lee Strobel, *The Case for the Real Jesus*

Jesus lived a sinless life for about thirty-three years on Earth. He had to be sinless because the sacrifice had to be without blemish.

> [5] You know that he was revealed to take away our sins, and in him is no sin. 1 John 3:5 WEB

He was born about 4-3 B.C. (the calendar did not start at the right place initially when people decided to use His birth as a reference point). His ministry was about three years long and began when He was about thirty. He was **crucified** around 30 A.D.

Before His crucifixion, Jesus was transfigured, and appeared with Moses and Elijah.

> [1] After six days, Jesus took with him Peter, James, and John his brother, and brought them up into a high mountain by themselves. [2] He was transfigured

before them. His face shone like the sun, and his garments became as white as the light. ³ Behold, Moses and Elijah appeared to them talking with him.

⁴ Peter answered, and said to Jesus, "Lord, it is good for us to be here. If you want, let's make three tents here: one for you, one for Moses, and one for Elijah."

⁵ While he was still speaking, behold, a bright cloud overshadowed them. Behold, a voice came out of the cloud, saying, "This is my beloved Son, in whom I am well pleased. Listen to him."

⁶ When the disciples heard it, they fell on their faces, and were very afraid. ⁷ Jesus came and touched them and said, "Get up, and don't be afraid." ⁸ Lifting up their eyes, they saw no one, except Jesus alone.  Matthew 17:1-8 WEB

God used this event to show that Jesus was indeed the Son of God, the Messiah, the second person of the Trinity, God come in the flesh. He also showed them Jesus' superiority over the Law, represented by Moses, and the prophets, represented by Elijah. That becomes abundantly clear when God mildly rebukes the disciples by telling them to listen to Jesus, and even clearer when only Jesus is left standing there.

Jesus died on a cross to pay for our sin.

> [24] who his own self bore our sins in his body on the tree, that we, having died to sins, might live to righteousness; by whose stripes you were healed. 1 Peter 2:24 WEB

Israel had a system of sacrifices already in place to deal with sin, however it was insufficient because it did not deal with sin once and for all:

¹ For the law, having a shadow of the good to come, not the very image of the things, can never with the same sacrifices year by year, which they offer continually, make perfect those who draw near. ² Or else wouldn't they have ceased to be offered, because the worshipers, having been once cleansed, would have had no more consciousness of sins? ³ But in those sacrifices there is a yearly reminder of sins. ⁴ For it is impossible that the blood of bulls and goats should take away sins. ⁵ Therefore when he comes into the world, he says,

> "Sacrifice and offering you didn't desire,
> but you prepared a body for me.
> ⁶ You had no pleasure in whole burnt offerings and sacrifices for sin.
> ⁷ Then I said, 'Behold, I have come (in the

scroll of the book it is written of me)

to do your will, O God.'"

**⁸** Previously saying, "Sacrifices and offerings and whole burnt offerings and sacrifices for sin you didn't desire, neither had pleasure in them" (those which are offered according to the law), **⁹** then he has said, "Behold, I have come to do your will." He takes away the first, that he may establish the second, **¹⁰** by which will we have been sanctified through the offering of the body of Jesus Christ once for all. Hebrews 10:1-10 WEB

Jesus Christ the Messiah is shown in these verses as a sufficient sacrifice for sin, once for all. His eternal nature was sufficient to pay for sin for all mankind for eternity. Jesus rose from the dead on the third day.

> ³ For I delivered to you first of all that which I also received: that Christ died for our sins according to the Scriptures, ⁴ that he was buried, that he was raised on the third day according to the Scriptures, .... 1 Corinthians 15:3-4 WEB

It is important to note that the Jews counted partial days as full days. So, part of Friday (one day) plus Saturday (one day) plus part of Sunday (one day) equals three days.

Jesus appeared to many after His resurrection.

> ⁵ and that he appeared to Cephas, then to the twelve. ⁶ Then he appeared to over five hundred brothers at once, most of whom remain until now, but some have also fallen asleep. ⁷ Then he appeared to James, then to all the apostles, ⁸ and last of all, as to

the child born at the wrong time, he appeared to me also. 1 Corinthians 15:5-8 WEB

When He first appeared to His disciples, Thomas was not with them. They touched Him – He had a resurrected body, but it still had holes in His side where the spear drove in and His legs and arms where the nails went through. Thomas said he would not believe until he touched the wounds. A few days later, Jesus appeared again. He allowed Thomas to put His hands in some of the holes and told him to believe and not be unbelieving (John 20:25-27).

Jesus certainly had a physical body after His resurrection. He ate and drank with His disciples (Luke 24:43, Acts10:40-41).

In addition to showing Thomas His wounds, as described in the section above, Jesus gave His disciples many other convincing proofs for the forty days He was with them after the resurrection (Acts1:3).

Jesus commissioned his disciples and told them they would receive power when the Holy Spirit came upon them.

> [7] He said to them, "It isn't for you to know times or seasons which the Father has set within his own authority. [8] But you will receive power when the Holy Spirit has come upon you. You will be witnesses to me in Jerusalem, in all Judea and Samaria, and to the uttermost parts of the earth."
> Acts 1:7-8 WEB

Jesus was received into heaven and sat down at the right hand of God.

¹⁹ So then the Lord, after he had spoken to them, was received up into heaven, and sat down at the right hand of God.  Mark 16:19 WEB

The early church had a common confession about Jesus.

¹⁶ Without controversy, the mystery of godliness is great:
> God was revealed in the flesh,
>> justified in the spirit,
>>
>> seen by angels,
>>
>> preached among the nations,
>>
>> believed on in the world,
>>
>> and received up in glory.  1 Timothy 3:16 WEB

In the passage above, justification in the Spirit refers to Jesus' **resurrection**, and the proclamation and belief refer to **evangelism** and **salvation**.

Jesus is the only way to salvation.

> ⁶ Jesus said to him, "I am the way, the truth, and the life. No one comes to the Father, except through me. John 14:6 WEB

"No one comes to the Father but through Me" means He is the only way. It is like having just one door to a house – those trying to come in another way will not be able to do so. It also shows that God requires that justice be done. Though mercy is greater than justice, justice is an integral part of God's unchanging character and His unchanging requirement.

When we **repent** of sin in order to be saved, we are also putting aside any other way of having a relationship with God, including among other things any other understanding of who God is and any other religion and its teachings. We also recognize that our own works cannot save us, especially knowing that breaking one of God's commands – without Jesus – is enough to send us to hell.

If people obey Jesus Christ the Messiah by following Him as Lord and Savior, He calls them friends.

> [14] You are my friends, if you do whatever I command you. [15] No longer do I call you servants, for the servant doesn't know what his lord does. But I have called you friends, for everything that I heard from my Father, I have made known to you. John 15:14-15 WEB

Though Jesus is speaking to the disciples, these words also apply to Christians who came after them, who also do what He commands. Though we still serve Him –

He is God – He calls us friends. He makes the things of God known to us, takes care of us, protects and blesses us. He listens and cares. He also has the power to help us and relieve the burden of suffering.

The Holy Spirit is the third person of the Trinity. He is listed third whenever the whole Trinity is mentioned in the New Testament. An example follows:

> [19] Go, and make disciples of all nations, baptizing them in the name of the Father and of the Son and of the Holy Spirit, …. Matthew 28:19 WEB

Though He is a spirit, He is fully a person of the Trinity. He is not simply the spirit of the Father or the Son. He is His own person, fully God, with all the attributes of God.

The Holy Spirit took part in creation.

> ² The earth was formless and empty. Darkness was on the surface of the deep and God's Spirit was hovering over the surface of the waters. Genesis 1:2 WEB

Though the exact action of the Holy Spirit is not described here, the Hebrew text describes the action of the Holy Spirit in terms of brooding, much like a bird broods over eggs before the baby birds hatch. There is a sense of preparation and care in the actions of the Holy Spirit.

The Holy Spirit indwells a Christian upon salvation. It is similar to what happened to the disciples after the resurrection.

> ²⁰ When he had said this, he showed them his hands and his side. The disciples therefore were glad when they saw the Lord. ²¹ Jesus therefore said to them again, "Peace be to you. As the Father has sent me,

even so I send you." **²²** When he had said this, he breathed on them, and said to them, "Receive the Holy Spirit! John 20:20-22 WEB

Note that the disciples first believed, then recognized Him as Lord, then received a commission to tell others about God, and finally received the Holy Spirit, who indwelt them (Ezekiel 36:27, 1 Corinthians 3:16).

The Holy Spirit convicts of sin, righteousness and judgment. Conviction in this sense is much like pointing out or making us aware, even multiple times if we have forgotten or wandered away from truth.

> **⁸** When he has come, he will convict the world about sin, about righteousness, and about judgment; **⁹** about sin, because they don't believe in me; **¹⁰** about righteousness, because I am going to my Father, and you won't see me any more; **¹¹** about

judgment, because the prince of this world has been judged. John 16:8-11 WEB

The above descriptions of God are often understandable to Muslims, but hard to accept. They often have the same three main questions about Christianity:

1. The virgin birth – how could someone be born of a woman with no male physical contact?
2. The Trinity – how could three be one and one be three?
3. The main one - was Jesus the son of God? How can a man be God?

# 4 HOW I CAME TO UNDERSTAND THE TRUTH OF THE GOSPEL – AND FOUND AN EVANGELISM METHOD THAT WORKS WITH MUSLIMS

The following is the journey that God led me through in order to answer my questions and provide me with the understanding needed for me to follow Jesus as Lord and Savior. It is quite detailed because many MBBs I know came to similar understandings in similar ways, also leading to following Jesus. My journey follows a pattern that can be employed to help Muslim seekers come to know the Lord. I have used the pattern successfully with Muslims, and others who have learned it have successfully used it and seen Muslims come to the Lord by the Lord's grace.

## 4.1 I HAD THREE QUESTIONS BEFORE BECOMING A CHRISTIAN

When I was a Muslim, I had three main questions about Christianity:

1. The virgin birth – how could someone be born of a woman with no physical contact?
2. The Trinity – how could three be one and one be three?
3. The main one - was Jesus the son of God? How can a man be God?

God began to answer my questions after I prayed this simple prayer: God, please show me who you are and I will follow you. I prayed it immediately after seeing the movie, *Star Wars*. Though I enjoyed the movie, the premise of a creative force in the universe was weak. The three major religions were more plausible, but I knew that they did not agree on the nature of God, so I decided to ask the source.

## 4.2  I KNEW GOD EXISTED

I was fairly sure that God existed. Among other things was the issue of first cause – where did the stuff come from that made us? The idea of starting from an explosion of stuff creating the universe was unsatisfactory to me. Again, where did the stuff come from? It had to come from somewhere, and something had to create it because science says that left to itself, everything tends to disorder. The universe was organized, and life on Earth was becoming more complex, not less. The only satisfactory first cause I could think of was God.

Another reason for the existence of God was the evidence of intelligence in the universe. There was order and what seemed to be intelligent design. Just the existence of order violates the second law of Thermodynamics, which essentially states that everything tends to disorder. The repeated patterns of design and different species, though explained by microevolution could not answer the issue of first cause, and there seem to be too much order for random events to be the reason for the order.

When I was nine, I participated in a science demonstration conducted by a professor who visited my school. He dissected a live frog in a humane manner. At the end of the dissection, he cut out the heart and placed it in my hand, where it continued to beat for about two minutes with no support from the rest of the body. At that point, I knew I wanted to study science and also knew that there was a God. The systems that God had created were so brilliant that there was built-in redundancy. The heart had its own pace maker. That is a redundant system. Part of the brain controls the heart, but also a local pacemaker for safety. Random events might have led to efficiency, but would be very unlikely to include a redundant system.

## 4.3 I FELT THAT GOD WOULD REMAIN A MYSTERY

At nine, I knew that God existed, but also knew that His full nature would likely remain a mystery to me. All around me were clues of his goodness. The beauty of nature, the variety of colors, and human individuality made me understand that God loved us and provided variety for us to experience and enjoy. Another reason to be sure that God was good was that he gave man a keen intelligence to enjoy life and to seek Him.

## 4.4 MY CONCEPT OF GOD PRIOR TO BECOMING A CHRISTIAN

Prior to Christianity, my concept of God was that He was one essence, one person. I did not like the idea of the Trinity because I thought that there were three absences, three people, therefore three guards. I also had a concept of God that lined up with the guard portrayed in the Old Testament – that God was compassionate and just, all-powerful, all-knowing, and many other good things. He was also one. I could not imagine polytheism being real. Different essences would lead in different directions, meaning that there could not truly be a unified set of values and standards which could be followed by anyone who was sane.

## 4.5 THE THREE MAIN RELIGIONS, ISLAM, JUDAISM, AND CHRISTIANITY, CANNOT BE RECONCILED WITH EACH OTHER

The three main religions, Islam, Judaism, and Christianity seem to portray a good God who loved people. I could not conceive that God would create people except for love. He wanted to show them love. He did not need to love anyone but wanted to love mankind.

However, though all three religions claim to have roots in the Old Testament, I could not reconcile them. Islam taught mercy, Christianity taught mercy but seemed to have three gods, and Judaism had one God but it seemed to rely on man approaching God through good works rather than God bringing man to himself. The only religion that did not rely on good works to relate to God was Christianity, but that seemed to be essentially polytheistic even though the New Testament stated that God was one.

Also, Islam belittled Christianity for having three gods. Islam explicitly denies that Jesus is the Son of God. Judaism teaches that the Messiah has not yet come, while Christianity teaches that he came about two thousand years ago. The concepts in the three religions could not be reconciled by me or by anyone else to my satisfaction. I knew I would have to choose one religion over the others.

## 4.6 STAR WARS

I had watched *Star Wars* just before going to college. As mentioned earlier, I asked God to show me who He was, telling him that I would follow him. I said that prayer just as I walked out of the movie theater. He answered the three main questions that I had after a period of about nine months. While the change was a journey, my experience of the change happened essentially in one afternoon. Though I did not become a Christian that afternoon, all of my questions were answered. It started with asking myself if Christianity could even be true.

## 4.7 MY FIRST QUESTION ANSWERED – THE VIRGIN BIRTH

My first question was about the virgin birth. Just by observation, and even at a young age, I knew that God could do anything. If he wanted to, he could certainly put a human being inside a virgin without a man having sex with her. That would be easy for the One who created the universe. Yes, I thought, that could be done.

## 4.8 MY SECOND QUESTION ANSWERED – THE TRINITY

My second question about Christianity was the apparent contradiction between the Father, the Son, and the

Holy Spirit and the claim that all three were God but that there was only one God. I realized my experience of "person" – one essence, one set of attributes, one entity, one identity - did not have to apply to God. He is a mystery. He does not need to conform to my experience or understanding. He is God, and does not have to follow my rules.

I realized the following could be true:

> God is one God. He has one set of attributes, one identity, one essence, but three entities. These three are persons in that they recognize the other two as you (as opposed to me), while knowing they are the same. The way that the persons of the Trinity differ from my normal concept of "person" is that the entities – the persons of the Trinity – are three separate persons with a shared essence. Essence determines being. There is one being, Father, Son

and Holy Spirit (Mt. 28:19). They are each fully God with all the attributes of God, yet are together one God. The Father, Son and Holy Spirit are the one God of the Old Testament.

That line of thinking could answer my second question about how could God be three and one. He is three persons, one essence – one God.

I knew that the plural nature of God was not just a New Testament concept. The two most used Hebrew words for God in the Old Testament – Elohim (God) and Adonai (Lord) – were plural. Those words exist in plural forms in manuscripts that pre-date Christianity. They could not have been changed to try to validate Christian claims.

There was no way to reconcile the plurality of God with either Judaism or Islam. Only Christianity could accomplish that – three persons, one essence, one God.

## 4.9 MY THIRD QUESTION ANSWERED – JESUS IS THE SON OF GOD

Two of my three questions were answered – those parts of Christianity could be valid. I just had to determine whether Jesus was the Son of God, the Messiah, as He claimed to be – not the Muslim version that comes back with the Mahdi, but the one born of a virgin, the second person of the Trinity.

I realized that I had told God that if I understood the answers to all three of those questions that I had asked before, when I walked out of *Star Wars*, that I would follow Him. I did mean it, but I was now nervous. Islam taught that if you worship a man as God, you would go to hell. It would be a major sin to follow Jesus if I was wrong. I had to be very careful about accepting the answer to this final question: was Jesus the Son of God as He claimed in the New Testament?

As I pondered the nature of sin and how it would affect my relationship with God, I realized that no matter what, if God is just, breaking any part of his command should lead to spiritual death. In Islam, sin is dealt with by the mercy of God. He essentially lets his mercy take care of my sin, as long as my good deeds outweigh my bad deeds. I had often wondered how this could be, knowing that God is just. My thought then, as it is now, is that a just God would require penalty for sin, not simply be merciful to the sinner. No amount of good deeds should be able to wipe out those transgressions, because there is still sin that has to be paid for. Otherwise, God is not acting in a just manner. He might as well not give commands. He might as well simply accept anyone.

Judaism has a right concept of a just God – saying there remains a penalty even in the light of God's mercy. That penalty must be paid for with a life, and in Judaism, an animal sacrifice counts as a substitute. However,

Judaism also contained a set of laws that really could not be fully carried out perfectly. There would always be the blemish of sin on the relationship because a human simply could not carry it out fully. The chilling part to me was that the only way to permanently satisfy a just God would be that God, an eternal life, would have to eternally pay for sin Himself to clear the relationship between Him and mankind of the blemish of sin, a blemish that could not be tolerated by a perfect, holy and just God. If he really did send his Son to do that, then that lavish gift would require a response. I would either have to accept the gift and follow Him, or reject it and then be rightly out of His good graces when I die. Yes, that would mean I would go to hell.

I was not yet ready to believe that Jesus was who He said He was. God had answered my third and final question – the gift of Jesus would be the only way to properly deal with sin and give mankind a chance to reverse the wrong committed by Adam. That would be true if Jesus was the Son of God, God in the flesh. I knew man could not be God, but an all-powerful God could become man to identify with mankind and pay for our sins. If indeed He did, the only proper response would be to follow God fully, with Jesus Christ the Messiah as Lord and Savior. Otherwise, I could not know God and would go to hell.

I knew the stakes, but needed more proof. I was not blithely going to change my way of believing.

### 4.9.1.1.1 GOD'S CONFIRMATION

The morning after my afternoon consideration, I realized that the only thing that I really needed to do was to determine whether Jesus in fact was the Son of God. God provided the proof in spectacular fashion.

Several times I had been invited by friends to attend Bible studies. When I would go, it would be with the express purpose of bringing up some controversial topic to make the Christians fight each other and internally laugh at them. This time, God turned the tables on me – but I think He smiled with me rather than laughed at me. As I mentioned above, the three questions were all answered in one afternoon. That evening I attended a Bible study. The topic was the name of Jesus. My friend who was teaching the Bible study felt impressed that he needed to pray for me openly and claim my soul for the kingdom of God in Christ Jesus. He was absolutely sure that the impression was from God. (By the way, please do not imitate this unless you are absolutely sure that you were supposed to do so. The consequences of doing this wrong are potentially very bad). At the beginning of the Bible study, he prayed aloud God to bring me to the saving knowledge of his Son in Jesus' name. He claimed my soul for the kingdom of God in Christ Jesus. Nothing happened outwardly, but on the inside of me things were moving powerfully. I felt a strong and settled peace as well as a strong impression that I should accept Jesus Christ the Messiah as my Lord and Savior. Just the fact that my mind had switched so cleanly after essentially an unremarkable prayer showed me the power of Jesus' name. He had to be, I knew, who He said He was. I had not willingly arrived at that conclusion. It actually came to me, and I knew it was true. I was convinced that God was speaking to me.

However, a still, small voice spoke with in my spirit. It said, "Not here and not now. When you become a Christian, you will be challenged and asked who you were with. Do not do this now." All of this had happened in about a second from the time of the prayer. I did not move. My friend looked up in surprise that I had not given my heart instantly to Jesus – I talked with him later and confirmed that that was true. He truly was surprised. He was that sure that the impression was from God. In fact, he was so sure that he prayed the same exact prayer again at the end of the Bible study. I had the same reaction of wanting to become a Christian, but this time there was no still small voice. The only moments in which I wanted to become a Christian were during those two prayers. However, I knew it was not yet time.

    My internal dialogue the next morning was similar to that of the previous morning. I realized that my search had come to a point where all that remained was to discover whether Jesus was who He said He was. As I thought that, I reflected on the previous night. I remembered the demonstration of His power. Though subtle, the power of His name was evident. There was no overt gesture of power that was visible to anyone else. It was private, just for me in the middle of a crowded dorm room. That name would not have had that power had Jesus not been God in the flesh. No man's name that I knew I had even come close to moving my mind that way as well as my heart and my being. I knew that I had my answer, and that Jesus was who He said He was. I decided that I would follow Him that day.

A little background. For the past three months, I had been attending a New Testament class at my university. It was required. However, during every class, either something that the professor would say or something from the New Testament would apply directly to my life. It would either speak to a specific situation I was in, or directly answer a question that I had in my mind. I asked God to confirm my decision during that class.

I was excited to get to class, thinking that I would get a confirmation and then follow Jesus Christ as my Lord and Savior. I asked God for a confirming verse in class, something that would directly relate to my potential decision. However, on the way to class an idea crept into my mind. I can now identify it as a temptation from the evil one. I fell for it. I knew that God could speak to me through the Bible. I asked him to confirm that the Bible was really His word in the following manner: I would open the Bible, put my finger down, and that verse would tell me to accept Jesus as Lord. After all, though satisfying my conditions seemed impossible, He was God, wasn't He? If He did so, then I would follow him. To make it worse, I decided that I would open the Bible in the middle. I thought there was no direct reference in that part of the Bible to Jesus.

What happened next, I can only describe as the sublime mercy of God. I arrived a little early and opened my Bible in the middle. I thought I had made it impossible for God to prove to me that Jesus was God in the flesh – there was no reference directly to the name "Jesus" in the Old Testament. That name occurs 990 times in the New Testament, but not in the Old Testament. I also knew that only about the last third of the Bible was the New Testament.

I put my finger on the page and began to read the following to my utter shock and horror. God had outsmarted the evil one, and gave me another chance.

⁹ For it is a rebellious people, lying children, children who will not hear Yahweh's law; ¹⁰ who tell the seers, "Don't see!" and to the prophets, "Don't prophesy to us right things. Tell us pleasant things. Prophesy deceits. ¹¹ Get out of the way. Turn aside from the path. Cause the Holy One of Israel to cease from before us." ¹² Therefore thus says the Holy One of Israel, "Because you despise this word, and trust in oppression and perverseness, and rely on it; ¹³ therefore this iniquity shall be to you like a breach ready to fall, swelling out in a high wall, whose breaking comes suddenly in an instant. ¹⁴ He will break it as a potter's vessel is broken, breaking it in pieces without sparing, so that there won't be

found among the broken piece a piece good enough to take fire from the hearth, or to dip up water out of the cistern." ¹⁵ For thus said the Lord Yahweh, the Holy One of Israel, "You will be saved in returning and rest. Your strength will be in quietness and in confidence." You refused, ¹⁶ but you said, "No, for we will flee on horses"; therefore you will flee; and, "We will ride on the swift"; therefore those who pursue you will be swift. ¹⁷ One thousand will flee at the threat of one. At the threat of five, you will flee until you are left like a beacon on the top of a mountain, and like a banner on a hill. ¹⁸ Therefore Yahweh will wait, that he may be gracious to you; and therefore he will be exalted, that he may have mercy on you, for Yahweh is a God of justice. Blessed are all those who wait for him. Isaiah 30:9-18 WEB

God had confronted my sin of trying not to hear, and told me of dire consequences if I continued in that way. I also understood that He was waiting to be gracious to me, and felt that He was going to show me something if I would repent and then turn to the New Testament and do the same thing as I had done in the Old Testament. However, I knew that this time I needed to be open rather than play games. Please do not do as I did by pointing to verses yourselves. It is not a good way to approach God, and looking back I realize that I tested Him, something that is forbidden. He was very gracious and forgiving to me. The Bible's answers come to us through reading, study and contemplation guided by the Holy Spirit.

In my Bible, as in most, was a page that divides the New Testament from the Old Testament. The page is like the title page of a book and contains no verses. I turned to it, then flipped a few pages and put down my finger without looking at the page. I landed on the following verse:

> [27] All things have been delivered to me by my Father. No one knows the Son, except the Father; neither does anyone know the Father, except the Son, and he to whom the Son desires to reveal him. Matthew 11:27 WEB

It was clear. The verse indicates that Jesus is the Son of the Father, and the only way to know God. I flipped again without looking at the words on the page, and randomly put my finger down. This time I was in John 1.

> [1] In the beginning was the Word, and the Word was with God, and the Word was God. John 1:1 WEB

This verse talks about Jesus as the Word of God. It also says He is God. I randomly slid my hand down the page and put my finger down without looking, thinking that the mathematical chances were astronomical that the next verse would still point so clearly to answering my third question: Was Jesus the Son of God?

> [14] The Word became flesh, and lived among us. We saw his glory, such glory as of the one and only Son of the Father, full of grace and truth.   John 1:14 WEB

This verse clearly says that Jesus is God's only begotten – by clear implication His Son. There was no sex involved. God, the One who can do anything, put Him inside a virgin. Man cannot be God, but God did become man. The Word – Jesus – was God and became flesh. I already knew the logic, but now I had confirmation. I had felt His power the night before. He had answered my questions, but I wanted to be especially sure. I did the same type of things seventeen more times for a total of twenty. Each verse I landed on told me that Jesus was who He said He is and pointed towards following Jesus Christ the Messiah as Lord and Savior. By the way, I know the Bible much better now than I did then. I cannot reproduce those results that I got on that day. I cannot even land on a relevant verse unless I look. That day I did not look for the verses and put my finger on verses in a row.

### 4.10 MY SALVATION

Now I knew that Jesus was the Son of God. I knew that I had to respond to the gift of Jesus or be separated from God. I wanted to obey quickly, and prayed a prayer for salvation (*see below*).

I prayed the prayer, on the advice of a wise man, by myself. It was good that I did, because the very first thing that my parents asked me when I told them that I was a Christian was, "Who were you with?"

The patterns above can help you prepare for sharing the gospel with Muslims, but more preparation is still needed.

# 5 PREPARING YOUR KNOWLEDGE BASE

To prepare your knowledge base, even if you are an MBB, please use this book and my book *Discipling Muslim Background Believers* to your advantage. They can provide you with useful information. The sections in *Discipling Muslim Background Believers* are relatively short, are practical and some sections also include MBB testimonies and advice which can give you insights into the Muslim mindset. Section 2 addresses some difficult circumstances that MBBs may face after conversion, which can give you further insights into different types of Muslim communities and how various responses to the gospel are often connected to levels of openness. Knowing these things will help you determine how to approach the Muslim to whom you are intending to minister.

Section 1 of *Discipling Muslim Background Believers* also contains a very useful, short table describing some of the **major differences between the Quran and the Bible**. A much longer table, not in section 1, shows the impact of Quranic substitution on the message of the Quran. It is in an appendix called **List of Major Quranic Substitutions**. Understanding this table will help a Christian know that though the Quran contains peaceful verses and verses favorable towards Christianity, those verses are no longer given effect. The principle of **substitution** is the reason, which essentially means that later verses affect or substitute the meaning of related verses given earlier.

Another thing to prepare is your own story of salvation and growth in Christ. To tell your story, it is often best to describe how things were before following Jesus Christ the Messiah as Lord and Savior, then explain how He led you to Himself, and finally describe the changes that you have noticed.

The reason to prepare is so that you have the ability to tell your story well, and within the time that you expect to be sharing. I find it useful to rehearse telling the essentials of Christianity (*see* 7.2 below) – the gospel, the good news of Christ – in various time frames. If I meet someone on a bus, I might want to tell the essentials within thirty seconds and be prepared for their response. To do that, I would need to have memorized not only the prayer for salvation, but also the steps that the new Christian should take. It is fairly difficult to go that fast, to sound comfortable while you are doing it, and to remember everything that you want to say. If possible, record yourself and listen to the recording. Then refine your delivery. Keep cycling through the process until satisfied. Please also be ready for the three- to five-minute opportunity to share the gospel, as well as a full opportunity in which you can take the time to explain and dialogue more with the seeker.

# 6   **SOME MORE EVANGELISM METHODS**

During a discussion, Muslims may try to discredit the Bible, saying it does not reflect the original message. If they do not accept your counter-arguments, consider changing the evangelism method, especially if it is very dependent on the quoting the Bible. The reason is that Muslims will not believe arguments premised on a book they view as false. Some apologists urge breaking through this problem with archeological proofs, a method which has been successful with only some Muslims. The danger is alienating the Muslim to the point of polite tolerance rather than listening to you. That happened to me many times. I simply used to let people finish trying to change me, not believing a word. The Lord had to use methods on me that did not rely on Bible quotes (*see below*). These methods have since been used successfully by me in sharing with other Muslims, and by other people to whom I taught them.

As a reminder, Muslims often have questions about three topics in Christianity:

1. The virgin birth,
2. The Trinity, and
3. The divinity of Jesus.

When discussing the divinity of Jesus with a Muslim seeker, it is helpful to ask them, if you feel **led by the Holy Spirit**, to sincerely pray to God to show the seeker who Jesus is. The seeker should understand that the true indicator of sincerity is to tell God that the seeker will follow Jesus if he or she discovers that Jesus is divine.

Many MBBs that I know prayed this prayer in one form or another, leading them to salvation. I did as well. I believe that God will answer this prayer if the seeker prays it sincerely. Please understand that the result may not be immediate. Nine months passed between the time that I prayed that prayer and the time that God convinced me to pray the prayer for salvation.

If the Muslim is a receptive to the gospel, does not immediately discredit the Bible, and is asking questions, use any evangelism method that you feel comfortable using. It is often helpful to practice on Christian friends or at least practice aloud by yourself before actually using the method with a Muslim. If the person is open to listening to things from the Bible, one of the more effective evangelism methods is Evangelism Explosion. Also consider using the short table containing some of the **major differences between the Quran and the Bible** as well as the much longer table that shows the **impact of Quranic substitution on the message of the Quran**. These tables make the choice between the two religions very clear, and can draw the Muslim to Christ. Please be very sensitive to the leading of the Holy Spirit because, used prematurely or wrongly, these tables could offend the Muslim even though the tables are true. Most Muslims are unaware of the actual message of the Quran and have been misinformed about Christianity.

Muslims are especially drawn to the love of God. They will see it when they see Christians truly love and when it is shown to them. Being their friend – not just for the sake of evangelism – is very attractive to them as you show them the love of Christ. Many MBBs that I know say they were drawn to Christ in a significant way by seeing God's love lived out.

Hospitality is a big part of Muslim culture. Your hospitality can have a major impact on a Muslim. They will see and feel your love, a very powerful testimony.

As a Muslim, I wanted to understand if Jesus really was who He said He was. One of the biggest proofs was seeing evidence of His work in the lives of others. Some of the strongest pieces of evidence I saw was my Christian friends in college loving each other. The way they cared for each other and served each other was selfless, and I knew that was not normal. I sensed something good had to be at work in their lives, and felt strongly that it was only through divine influence. The awareness of having seen divine influence was confirmed by reading the Bible and seeing that their actions were consistent with the life of Jesus – strong evidence to me that Jesus was who He said He was.

Be open to following the Lord, even if He asks you to do something strange. Of course, be sure that you are **hearing God**. An example follows. After I had walked with Jesus as my Lord and Savior for about two years, He gave me a ministry to poor people in jail. People were getting saved at a rate of about 200 per year (for about three years of jail ministry). It goes without saying that it was God who was saving people, not me. I was simply sharing the gospel with them. I was still in university at the time. God had already granted many of my desires to see people come to know Him, but I still wanted to see Muslims come to know Him and experience the joy that I knew they would have if they knew Him in Christ.

I was in class one morning, waiting for the professor to arrive. On the front page of the school paper was a picture of a man accused of conspiring to kill three people. By his name alone I knew that he was a Muslim. I begin to pray for his salvation, and felt impressed that I was to share the gospel with him in the jail. The man was in the jail in which I ministered, but I was only allowed to minister in it in once a week, and I had already used up that week's session. I tried to get special permission to see just him, discussing possible ways to go see him with the policeman at the intake desk for about fifteen minutes. The policeman refused. As I was leaving, the Lord reminded me that He had told me to not turn back. I tried to reason with the Lord, saying that I had done my best. The Lord simply stated again that He had told me to not turn back.

After being told the second time, I realized that I was disobeying and repented. As soon as I could, I turned my car around and returned to the jail, thinking that God would have done a miracle and had somebody else at the desk even though shift change was hours away. To my dismay, the same man was at the desk – but I knew that God had spoken to me. I was going to try again regardless of the outcome. I walked up to the same policeman that it turned me away and simply asked if I could go see that specific gentleman. Without batting an eyelid, he said, "Sure." I was stunned. I realized as I approached the proper jail cell that God had indeed performed a miracle, but differently than I had expected. The policeman acted as if I had not been talking with him for fifteen minutes already about the same issue, and that he had repeatedly said no.

  I had only been allowed five minutes with the prisoner, and by God's grace was able to share the gospel and pray a prayer for salvation with a man who was eventually convicted for his part in killing three innocent people. This salvation was extremely significant for him, but also for me. I had always felt the desire to minister to Muslims, and was able to see that sharing the gospel with a Muslim and seeing good results was not difficult. It encouraged me in my desire to minister to Muslims.

By God's grace, I have had the opportunity to minister to Muslims. I have seen more than fifty Muslims saved and discipled. I did not have the opportunity to disciple all of them, only some of them. The others were discipled by trusted individuals. I also led or co-led a weekly local ministry that reached out to refugees, some of whom were Muslim. At a different time, I taught a class at church regarding ministry to Muslims. I have also ministered to Muslims as an assistant leader in an evangelistic Bible study for international university students.

I had good results in the above ministry times, confirming that God was working through me to Muslims. I continued to wait until the calling was confirmed through other people recognizing it and God showing me through scripture and impressions that indeed I was called to minister to Muslims. I encourage any MBBs to hear the Lord about their calling, but also to be wise, to seek wise counsel, and to use wisdom in determining their calling. Trusting in hearing God is not the same as trusting in God. In other words, please do not solely rely on your ability to hear God in order to determine your calling. Allow God to use various methods, including confirmation through others and circumstances to confirm what you think that you are hearing.

One pitfall to avoid is expecting to see all of Christ in a single person, nor to be all of Christ to any individual. Even though I could see the likeness of Christ being formed in my Christian friends, no single one of them carried

Christ's entire image. It was seeing many Christians loving each other and me that showed me much of Christ in them. I could see that He was transforming them, and recognized that I could not expect any one of them to be perfect. Neither do you have to be perfect to be effective in sharing the gospel.

Before I became a Christian, people at the university I attended knew that I was a Muslim. Some of my Christian friends zealously desired that I become a Christian. In their zeal, they did not use the best of methods. At first, they simply tried to argue with me. When they were not trying to convince me, they really did not pay much attention to me. I am very independent, and did not need attention, but I was examining their conduct to try to find out if Christ was who He said He was. I was searching for the truth at the time. However, they did not know that. One day, after they had confronted me with the Bible, I told them that they would be much more effective if they actually started living the way that they believed and loved me rather than trying to force me to become a Christian. I also said I felt that they were trying to cram the Bible down my throat rather than reason with me, and their entire approach lacked love. I told them, not wanting sympathy but to tell them the truth, that their approach made me feel like I was to them simply an object to be converted – a potential notch on the belt – rather than a person. I also told them that if becoming a Christian would make me treat people like that, I did not want to become a Christian. I thought that would be the end of their attempts to convert me.

Thankfully, my words had the opposite effect. I later found out what they did was to listen to what I had said, to realize that they needed to change how they were doing things, and to spend some time in repentance and asking God to show them how to love me properly. They started including me in things that they were doing and genuinely showed care and concern for me as a person. I started to see Christ in them instead of people who were trying to convert me. Seeing the change as they begin to actually live out their faith was a powerful testimony to me, and part of the reason that I continued to seek understanding regarding the nature of Jesus. When sharing the gospel, please show the love of God to the people you are talking with, even if it is just for a few seconds. That love will be remembered, and is an extremely powerful way of drawing people to Christ. It is also part of obeying the Lord.

Many Muslims are being saved through divine encounters, including: dreams of Jesus telling them to follow Him as Lord and Savior; visions of Jesus telling them the same thing; and encounters with Jesus telling them to talk to a specific Christian who could tell them the gospel and pray a prayer for salvation with them. A suggested prayer is to ask God that the Muslims around you would have divine encounters with God and that you would have divinely directed encounters with Muslims who are on their journey to follow Jesus. Be open to what the Lord will do, leave the results to Him and praise and thank Him for good results.

Some additional practical steps:

If you share the gospel with a Muslim and they refuse to pray the prayer for salvation, ask them if at least they will ask God to show them who Jesus really is (with the sincere understanding that they will follow Him if they discover He is God). This prayer is a common element in the salvation of many MBBs that I know.

If the Muslim demonstrates a curiosity for Christ, listens, asks questions and seems open to learning more, treat them as a seeker. As led by the Lord, use the reading path in the Introduction of *Discipling Muslim Background Believers*, the seeker Bible study (*see* my book *Muslim Seeker Bible Study*); and determine whether the Muslim is willing to join a seeker **small group**. This group may need to meet secretly and use secret communication methods as **secret believers**.

# 7  CONSIDERATIONS FOR THE SEEKER

There are many things for the seeker to consider. Some of them follow.

## 7.1  ASK FOR REVELATION

One of the seeker's considerations is to decide if they truly want to know God's nature and follow Him. If they are sincere, they should ask God to show them. I believe He will answer that prayer. The seeker should be aware that sometimes prayers are not answered instantly – the answer sometimes takes time. My answer took nine months, some MBBs are answered in seconds, and I know a few who were answered in years.

The seeker needs to become very familiar with some essential Christian beliefs.

## 7.2 BECOME FAMILIAR WITH ESSENTIAL CHRISTIAN BELIEFS

These are some essential Christian beliefs:

1. There is one God. He is both one essence and three persons at the same time – He is a triune God, at the same time Father, Son and Holy Spirit – the **Trinity**.
2. **God** is good, and He is a rewarder of those who seek him.

> [6] Without faith it is impossible to be well pleasing to him, for he who comes to God must believe that he exists, and that he is a rewarder of those who seek him. Hebrews 11:6 WEB

3. **Jesus** the Messiah has come in the flesh.
4. Jesus was born of a virgin and is therefore both God and man.
5. He died on a cross for all of our **sins**, and our individual **forgiveness** can only come if we ask Jesus Christ the Messiah to be our Lord and Savior.
6. He rose again on the third day to give us new life.
7. If we **repent** of our sins and turn to Jesus Christ the Messiah as our Lord and Savior, we will be **born again**, know God, and be with Him forever.
8. Jesus is the only way to **salvation**, and a Christian cannot follow Jesus and another belief system, person or religion – it is an exclusive relationship. No other religion means that we will follow and obey Him as our sole source of

salvation. We will follow no other way of approaching or knowing God or having eternal life in heaven.

9. Jesus Christ is coming again and will come and get living Christians, **resurrect** dead Christians, give us new bodies, make us His bride, and spend eternity with us.

A person who prays for salvation should believe the above before praying for salvation.

The seeker may be quite interested in knowing what type of things he or she might be expected to do if he or she decides to follow Jesus Christ the Messiah as Lord and Savior.

## 7.3 WHAT DOES BEING A CHRISTIAN LOOK LIKE?

Christians will have good fruit in their lives (John 14). They will perform good works as a result of **salvation**, but the works do not save them (Ephesians 2:4-10) but rather confirm their faith (James 2:14-20). The works are a result of being in a relationship with God. The following list covers many of the main points, but is not exhaustive:

1. Getting **baptized in water**
2. Getting **baptized in the Holy Spirit**.
3. Confessing Jesus as Lord before men.

> [32] Everyone therefore who confesses me before men, him I will also confess before my Father who is in heaven. [33] But whoever

denies me before men, him I will also deny before my Father who is in heaven.

Matthew 10:32-33 WEB

4. **Loving God and people** (Mark 12:29-31)**.**
5. **Praying** for others and yourself
6. **Loving your enemies** (*see* Matthew 5:43-48, Matthew 10:34-36).
7. Growing in **intimacy with God.**
8. Growing as a disciple (refer to **Reading Path for MBB Discipleship**).
9. **Repenting** when you **sin** against God and people, **forgiving** people, asking for forgiveness from God and people, and receiving forgiveness.
10. Committing to **seek first His kingdom**, a spiritual one, and His righteousness (Matthew 6:33).

11. **Reading, studying and understanding the Bible**.
12. Enjoying the benefits of **being in God's family** and having the benefits of **righteousness** and the new covenant.
13. Living by **faith**.
14. **Hearing God** and **being led by the Holy Spirit**.
15. Knowing and using your **spiritual gifts**.
16. Being fruitful (John 14) and walking in righteousness by **grace through faith**.
17. Being **sanctified and transformed**.
18. Practicing **spiritual disciplines**.
19. **Keeping the sabbath**.
20. Repenting of and denying any other religion.
21. Avoiding **syncretism**.
22. **Finding God's plan for your life**.

23. Following God's specific **vision and leading** for your life – how He will fulfill His plan for you.
24. **Making disciples** that follow **essential Christian beliefs** and equipping them (refer to **Reading Path for MBB Discipleship**) to make more disciples (refer to **Reading Path for Evangelism**).
25. **Fellowshipping** directly with other believers if it is safe to do so, otherwise can use indirect methods such as phones or the internet.
26. Taking **communion**.
27. Serving the **church** through discipling others, participating in **small groups** and church, and helping it grow by finding your **spiritual gifts** and using them.
28. **Tithing and giving** generously.

29. Considering their lives lost for His sake (Matthew 10:38-39).

30. Being a **secret believer**, if necessary.

31. Enduring **persecution**.

32. Engaging in **spiritual warfare**.

33. Enduring to the end (Matthew 10:21-23) and not turning away from God (Luke 9:57-62, and 2 Timothy 2:12).

The things listed above will usually happen in a process and will take time.

A seeker should know and count the cost of a decision to follow Jesus Christ the Messiah as Lord and Savior.

## 7.4 COUNTING THE COST

There is a cost to following Jesus Christ the Messiah as Lord and Savior, and it is worth everything to know God. Some have been persecuted, including being disowned, disinherited, ostracized, tortured, imprisoned and killed for being Christians. Others have lost everything. Still others face little to no persecution.

The interesting thing is that people keep becoming Christians because of the great value of knowing God and being part of His family. He lives inside you, and shows you His care.

Not every Christian will face persecution, but all must be willing to do so. He gives grace to endure. There is also the option of being a **secret believer** for a period.

After counting the cost, the seeker may benefit from knowing a few of the significant differences between the Quran and the Bible.

## 7.5 SOME SIGNIFICANT DIFFERENCES BETWEEN THE QURAN AND THE BIBLE

In the comparison below, the parentheticals contain the chapter and verse of the Quran, and the Bible verse and more detailed explanation of the words or phrases in bold are in my book *Discipling Muslim Background Believers*.

Regarding God, the Quran speaks of one God (47.19), wholly other (42.11) and distant (6.103). He is perfect (4.171; 59:22-24), and, by implication, cannot suffer because He is perfect. The Bible speaks of one God in three persons, the **Trinity**, with one essence – Father, Son, and Holy Spirit. He is near, loves us, calls us into His family through **salvation**, lives in us (John 17:20-26), and suffers with us (Hebrews 4:15).

Regarding getting to heaven, the Quran speaks of having to do more good than bad (21.47; 7.8-9; 20.82;

66.8), and only God knows if they will make it there. The Bible states that Christians are certain they will go to heaven based on the **crucifixion** and **resurrection** of Christ, and if they follow Jesus Christ the Messiah as Lord and Savior unto **salvation**. Christians know their destination from the beginning, and their obedience flows from a relationship of **righteousness** – having good standing with God.

Regarding whom to love, the Quran speaks of loving the household of Islam, with instruction to convert or kill others (3.28; 5.51; 9.5; 9.23; 9.29; 9.113). Converts who are forced to convert are essentially second-class citizens because they have to live in subjection (9.29). The Bible speaks of **loving and serving** all people, even loving enemies (Matthew 5:44). Converts are on the same level as their evangelists – all children of God (John 1:12) with the full privileges of being His children (Galatians 4:7).

Regarding substitution in the holy book, the Quran changed as Muhammad moved from Mecca to Medina and became involved in more battles. The verses from the last five years of Muhammad's life, when he fought most, are the most warlike (*see* the Appendix **List of Major Quranic Substitutions**). Also, the Quran changed from no compulsion in religion (2.256) and consult the people of the Book (10.94-95) if you doubt what was revealed to compel their conversion or kill them (9.29; 9.5). The Bible's change from the Old Testament to the New Testament was prophesied for hundreds of years before it happened, and was planned before time began. The Bible also changed from an eye for an eye (exodus 21:24) to turn the other cheek (Matthew 5:38-42) and love your enemies (Matthew 5:43-48). Also, Jesus fulfilled rather than replaced the Law.

Regarding the nature of heaven, the Quran states that Muslims can indulge in things previously prohibited, such as many virgins (56.12-39). It does talk about having one's highest satisfaction in God (5.119). The Bible states that full satisfaction comes through relationship with God (Matthew 25:23, John 14:2-4, Revelation 21:4-8). There is no need for self-indulgence in heaven, nor is there any.

Regarding the main reasons for obedience, The Quran indicates that Muslims should obey because God is God, and they also need to do enough good works to get into heaven (*see above*). The Bible states that Christians should obey because God is God, and also because Christians are in relationship with Him, are in His family and He lives in them (*see above*) – His life in Christians causes a desire to do what He says and gives Christians the ability to do His will. Christians live and do good works by **grace through faith**.

Once the seeker knows all of the information in the chapters above and has come to a decision to follow Jesus

Christ as Lord and Savior, they can pray a prayer for salvation.

# 8  PRAYER FOR SALVATION

If a Muslim wants to pray the prayer of salvation, please make sure that you have covered with them **essential Christian beliefs** (*see above* in 7.2) to ensure that they believe them. Then they can pray the prayer for salvation.

This prayer, or something very similar to it, if prayed with belief and sincerity, will result in the greatest change in your life. You will have **salvation**. You will join the family of God, and He will be your Father forever.

Someone told me a before I prayed a similar prayer that it would be the greatest ride in my life and that I should sit back and enjoy it. That person was right. When you are ready, please pray the prayer below to God – you simply read it and agree to it.

Gracious God, thank You for your goodness towards me. I believe that You are Father, Son, and Holy Spirit. I believe that You sent Jesus Christ the Messiah, Your Son, to Earth. I believe that He was born of a virgin. I believe that He died on a cross to pay for the sins of the world, including mine. I believe that Jesus Christ the Messiah rose from the grave on the third day to give life to those who believe in Him and follow Him as Lord. I believe that Jesus Christ the Messiah will return. I turn away from all of my sin and ask that You would forgive me. I turn to You. I call Jesus Christ the Messiah my Lord and Savior, and ask that You, Father, Son and Holy Spirit would save me. I want to obey Jesus as God, and follow His teachings and those in the Bible. Thank You, Father, Son, and Holy Spirit, for saving me.

If you sincerely believed the essential Christian beliefs and sincerely prayed the above prayer or something similar to it, then you are now changed. You are **born again**, and are a part of God's family. You are saved, and are a Christian.

You do not need to keep praying this prayer. It is a solemn commitment that only needs to be lived out daily rather than made anew daily.

# 9 STEPS TO TAKE AFTER SALVATION

Here are some steps for the seeker to take after praying a prayer for salvation:

1. Get to know **God** better.

    1.1 Read the **Bible**.

    1.2 Communication and **intimacy with God**.

2. Get **baptized**.
3. Find **fellowship** if you can.
4. Take **communion**.
5. Seek the **baptism of the Holy Spirit**.
6. Follow the steps in the **Reading Path for MBB Discipleship**. It will suggest where and how to start your journey as a Christian.

I have also written a Bible study that complements the above reading path from my book *Discipling Muslim*

*Background Believers*. The book is called *Muslim Background Believer Bible Studies*.

The MBB should try to find a discipleship group or **small group**. This group may need to be secret, meet secretly, and use secret communication methods – circumstances may require that the MBB become a **secret believer** for a while. If so, my book *Discipling Muslim Background Believers* will be very useful because it contains guidance on preparing to be a secret believer, advice on avoiding syncretism, and guidance about living as a fruitful Christian while keeping faith secret from some or many people. It also helps decide when to stop living as a secret believer.

It is important to note that once a Muslim becomes an MBB, there may be a period during which they feel disoriented because the Quran is no longer their guide. The Quran is very specific about some daily tasks, whereas the Bible essentially provides principles. They will need help finding what the Bible says, and quickly. *Discipling Muslim Background Believers* has a helpful index containing concepts and words, and also a glossary. It can be a useful reference as the MBB grows in discipleship.

# **BOOKS**

### DISCIPLING MUSLIM BACKGROUND BELIEVERS

Abu Da'ud

This book can be purchased:
- From my website, abudaud.com, in EPUB and MOBI (Amazon Kindle format); or
- From Amazon in MOBI (Amazon Kindle format) or in paperback.

MUSLIM
BACKGROUND
BELIEVER
BIBLE STUDIES

Abu Da'ud

This book can be purchased:
- From my website, abudaud.com, in EPUB and MOBI (Amazon Kindle format); or
- From Amazon in MOBI (Amazon Kindle format) or in paperback.

# MUSLIM SEEKER BIBLE STUDY

Abu Da'ud

This book can be purchased:
- From my website, abudaud.com, in EPUB and MOBI (Amazon Kindle format); or
- From Amazon in MOBI (Amazon Kindle format) or in paperback.

OVERVIEW OF
DISCIPLESHIP
IN
DISCIPLING
MUSLIM
BACKGROUND
BELIEVERS

Abu Da'ud

This book can be purchased:
- From my website, abudaud.com, in EPUB and MOBI (Amazon Kindle format); or
- From Amazon in MOBI (Amazon Kindle format) or in paperback.

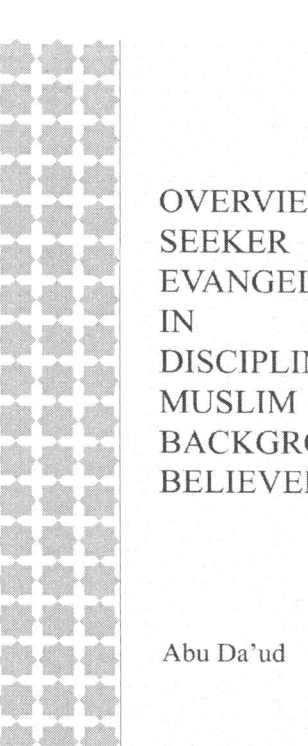

# OVERVIEW OF SEEKER EVANGELISM IN DISCIPLING MUSLIM BACKGROUND BELIEVERS

Abu Da'ud

This book can be purchased:
- From my website, abudaud.com, in EPUB and MOBI (Amazon Kindle format); or
- From Amazon in MOBI (Amazon Kindle format) or in paperback.

# **ABOUT THE AUTHOR**

Abu Da'ud is a former Muslim, born and raised in a Muslim majority country, with family members from both the Sunni and Shia branches of Islam. He was raised Sunni and was also taught Shia Islam. He is the only Christian known on either side of his family and has been a Christian for nearly forty years. His parents disowned and disinherited him once they discovered he became a Christian.

By God's grace, he did the ministry below and gives Him all the glory:
- Led more than 50 Muslims to the Lord
- Led over 1,000 people to the Lord
- Discipled Muslims and others
- Led
    - weekly refugee ministry for Muslim and MBBs
    - small groups
- Taught
    - Muslim ministry class at a large church (10,000+)
    - Bible study class for Muslim college students
    - Perspectives on the World Christian Movement course
- Started a small church

Made in United States
Orlando, FL
14 September 2024